UNLIKELY SAVIORS

Unlikely Saviors

Stan Stone

fmsbw

San Francisco, California

ISBN-13: 978-1-7362624-1-2

Cover artwork by William Salit

Author photo by William Salit

fmsbw

San Francisco, California

This book is dedicated to the men in my life,
who continue to inspire, instruct and influence:
William, Vincent, John Sr., John Jr., Kevin and Tracy.

CONTENTS

Preface: A Chorus in the Wings

PREFACE: A CHORUS IN THE WINGS

The proverbial stone tossed into water generates ripples. In Stan Stone's inaugural verse collection, we have a poet skipping his imagination across historical time and the span of felt experience to create concentric rings. These deeply personal layers cascade out as affecting set-pieces; read collectively, they begin to intertwine, creating a vivid, resonant tableau.

Unlikely Saviors begins with "Open Book." Here is the poet *"face to face"* with blank pages, witnessing words themselves appear to buoy and propel him to "reveal hidden secrets" visible "when held up to the light." Stone expands this classic scene of a poet invoking the muse, by casting himself as the metaphorical blank page itself. This role for the poet, as the *tabula rasa* upon which the other figures — the unlikely saviors — leave their marks, skillfully and subtly unifies and adds dimension to the collection.

Other poems introduce us to mother, father, ancestor, husband, childhood neighbors, and characters like the shape-shifting inner voice of the "ShouldaWouldaCoulda" and the luminous, mysterious "Ujvavl Prakaash." In all, Stone's clear voice rings through. We begin to know not only the details of his life, but the qualities of its tenderness, through lines like:

I am the son of a Black man
who embraced me
when I confessed to
loving another man.

Stone is also a playwright and an actor. His vocation comes through, adding to our understanding and appreciation of this body of work. As a poet, Stone inhabits the characters he creates and breathes life into them through verse. The book closes with the title poem. The voice in "Unlikely Saviors" begins in despair, "the sunken place/with no trace of who I am," until the presences (perhaps the saviors from all the poems that have come before) gallop in to dispel "the darkness." One feels the excitement of this finale as akin to the moment when the community of players come out on stage at the end of a performance. It's a culminating instant, in which all present feel as one, including Stone's reading audience. Bravo!

Tamsin Spencer Smith
San Francisco, 2020

OPEN BOOK

I find myself
between prologue
and epilogue.

Face to face
with blank pages
that reveal hidden secrets
when held up to the light.

Words appearing
as if by magic.

Urging me to gather my strength
and leap repeatedly from the precipice,
and fall into the waiting arms
of the muse.

LEAN IN

Lean into me

As a flower leans into the sun

Lean into me

As a runner leans into the run

I will be your container

When you long to be held

I will be your looking glass

When dragons need to be felled

So lean into me

As a flower leans into the sun

Lean into me

As a runner leans into the run

I AM THE SON OF A BLACK MAN

I am the son of a Black man
who pushes me to be strong
in the face of adversity.

I am the son of a Black man
who taught me to judge a man
by the content of his character.

I am the son of a Black man
who loved my mother
and told her so. Often.

I am the son of a Black man
who did not spare the rod,
resulting in an unspoiled child.

I am the son of a Black man
who embraced me
when I confessed to
loving another man.

I am the son of a Black man
who raised me to be polite
but not a pushover.

I am the son of a Black man
whose smile lights up a room
and warms my heart.

And when this man leaves this mortal earth
I will suffer a wound so deep, it cannot be healed.
But I will derive comfort in knowing
that this man lives on in me.

For I am the son of a Black man.

SUMMER

Heat rising in waves
from black tarred city streets.

Pig-tailed girls double-dutching
to an internal beat.

Scratchy sounds of the Phillies game
on a tiny transistor radio.

Persistent flies, hovering over lemonade, refusing to go.

Tee shirts sticking to young boy's backs
like cellophane.

Distant sounds of barking dogs,
fire engines, trains.

Fat black men with fat cigars
dangling perilously in their mouths.

Screen doors banging shut
as kids on a mission clamor to get out.

The snap and pop of chicken
frying in a cast iron pan.

A gaggle of women gossiping
in thin cotton dresses,
waving cardboard church fans.

Afros, wet with sweat,
Bobbing on animated heads

Babies napping
in their parent's unmade bed.

Wallpaper covered in flocked gold.
Tables covered in plates, trays, bowls.

Plastic wrapped sofa,
keeping the new from looking old.

Sitting on the stoop, watching the summer go by like a pitcher's
fast ball.

Giggly girls in short shorts
feigning indifference to catcalls.

Motown blasting on the stereo.
There's dancing in the streets.

It's summer in the city.
No reprieve from the heat.

SCRAP

She was draped like mirrors
after a death.

Jean Nate masked the memories
of cotton fields.

She wore the shell of modernity.

But in this moment,
she revealed herself.

Southern as bare feet.

Seasoned like fatback
in a pot of greens.

Salty like butter
on cornbread.

She lived her life
between the lines.

A lifetime of sighs.

A MOTHER'S LAMENT

You won't miss me.
My spotlight has dimmed.

I no longer walk on water
leaving miracles in my wake.

Only my eyes bear witness
to the final passion play.

I sit alone at the window
waiting to be witnessed.

I pressed my hair.
Got dressed in my Sunday best.

My mouth, a rose
floating in a dark and troubled sea.

My past, I wear
like rain-soaked wool.

Does my melancholy
cause you unease?

I embrace it all,
for God won't let me suffer.

Will you miss me?

Am I a dream
half forgotten?

YOU'D BETTA WORK

He had a sway
A natural fluidity you might say
An effortless unwrinkled silky stride
It was less of a walk
And more like a glide

Had nowhere to be
But he moved purposefully
Leaning into the human tide
His hips a rolling river
Side to side to side

He had a sway
Clearly written on his resume
A PHD in perpetual motion
Schooled in the art of self-devotion

Feet too small
Hips too wide
Thighs too sturdy for a man his size

Why you gotta walk that way?
Words he heard from day to day to day

He was proud and unapologetic
His gait was a fine esthetic
Cause God don't make ugly
His mom was known to say
You walk your walk, child
I loves you anyway

He had a sway
With head held high
To somehow portray
No fear
No doubt
No feet of clay

So don't get it twisted
Don't come double fisted
You picked the wrong man today
He ain't here to play
And you...well you
Best move out the way

THE SHOULDAWOULDACOULDA

The ShouldaWouldaCoulda crept in again last night

Challenging me with its unwavering stare

Even when it's not, it is always there

It is a shapeshifter

A talented grifter with time on its hands

It is a god resurrecting expired words and deeds

It is an earworm playing the same old tune

Repeat

Repeat

It is a heckler with a front row seat at the foot of the bed

It is my mother with words cutting deep inside my head

It is me just before sleep

It is me.

It is me.

THE MOMENT

Yesterday is gone
and tomorrow is yet to come.

I find peace in the in-between.

I am a falling leaf, looking neither at the heavens above
nor at the earth below.

Content to ride the wind.

UJVAAL PRAKAASH

The stars turned affectedly modest.
Decidedly demure.

The sun, sought anonymity
behind contemptuous clouds.

The moon was reduced to a
half-hearted crescent smile.

For it would be fools folly
to compete with
the brilliance of her.

Fawning fireflies gathered
to pay homage,
gleefully basking in her refulgence.

She is solidly transparent.
A prism with a lifetime of cracks.

Unshielded.

She retreats to the Cimmerian shade,
tending to her embers.

Emerging in full radiance.

Unguarded.

I see the wholeness of her.

ENTWINED

Entwined in a
complicated embrace

Mismatched spoons
Finding the places
Where they fit

A tangle of arms
And legs
Loosely knotted

Breath
Finding and loosing
Synchronicity

The days anguish
Put to rest

I embrace
The sleep
Of the innocents.

WILLIAM

We met

And I fell fast

Doomed to fall

Day after day

Deeper

Further

I have no choice

But to fall

Into you

UNLIKELY SAVIORS

The blackness of night
Crept unceremoniously into the day

I've settled into the sunken place
With no trace of who I am

Disconnected
Abstracted

On cue, they come
Like stampeding cattle

Rumbling
Crashing

With orchestrated bedlam
They come

A symphony of Gatling guns
Shattering the dark

Unlikely saviors

Lifting
Healing

Filling the empty spaces

Stan Stone, 2019

Stan Stone is an actor, sketch writer, short story author, director, and, more recently, a poet. Originally from Philadelphia, he's lived in San Francisco since 1985. Stone writes, directs, and performs with Barewitness, an award-winning improv-based filmmaking collective. His most recent play "Work in Progress" premiered in 2019, as part of the Queer as Fuck show at the Bindelstiff Theater.

Stone has said that his life—his real life—began with death. In 2005, Stan's caregiving work brought him to Maitri, a San Francisco hospice, where he cared for the chronically ill and dying. The most intimate moments would find him sitting at the bedside of the dying, providing quiet comfort and holding space. The work was moving, enlightening, and at times unexpectedly funny; but it was also emotionally exhausting. Writing and performing became necessary practices of self-care.

As a child, Stan wrote and drew superhero comic books for fun, and as a way to escape to a better world. That urge to channel and process his internal world became focused on the written word and daily journaling. When his mother passed in 2014, he wrote and performed a solo show about the experience, "Johnny & Scrap", which was originally mounted at the Studio Grand in Oakland in 2016.

THE PAGE POETS SERIES

www.ingramcontent.com/pod-product-compliance
Lightning Source LLC
Chambersburg PA
CBHW032008060426
42449CB00032B/1242